The Coconut Seller

Jack Scholes

About this Book

For the Student

🎧 Listen to the story and do some activities on your Audio CD

🎧 End of the listening excerpt

🗣 Talk about the story

ban° When you see the blue dot you can check the word in the glossary

P Prepare for Cambridge English: Preliminary (PET) for Schools

For the Teacher

 A state-of-the-art interactive learning environment with 1000s of free online self-correcting activities for your chosen readers.

Go to our Readers Resource site for information on using readers and downloadable Resource Sheets, photocopiable Worksheets and Answer Keys. Plus free sample tracks from the story.

www.helblingreaders.com
For lots of great ideas on using Graded Readers consult Reading Matters, the Teacher's Guide to using Helbling Readers.

Level 5 Structures

Modal verb *would*	Non-defining relative clauses
I'd love to ...	Present perfect continuous
Future continuous	*Used to / would*
Present perfect future	*Used to / used to doing*
Reported speech / verbs / questions	Second conditional
Past perfect	Expressing wishes and regrets
Defining relative clauses	

Structures from lower levels are also included.

NEW for Helbling Readers

Helbling Readers e-zone is the brand new state-of-the-art easy-to-use interactive learning environment from Helbling Languages. Each book has its own set of online interactive self-correcting cyber homework activities containing a range of reading comprehension, vocabulary, listening comprehension, grammar and exam preparation exercises.

Students test their language skills in a stimulating interactive environment. All activities can be attempted as many times as necessary and full results and feedback are given as soon as the deadline has been reached. Single student access is also available.

Teachers register free of charge to set up classes and assign individual and class homework sets. Results are provided automatically once the deadline has been reached and detailed reports on performance are available at a click.

1000s of free online interactive activities now available.

www.helbling-ezone.com

CONTENTS

Meet the Author

Dear Jack, tell us a little about yourself.
I was born in the North of England and studied German and Russian at Liverpool University. After graduation● I spent several years travelling around the world, teaching English to finance● the trips. I then went back to England to do a postgraduate● course at London University. I came to Brazil in 1976 and have lived and worked here, teaching and writing, ever since.

When did you start writing stories?
My first story was published in 1999. This is now my tenth book.

How do you think of your stories?
Stories are around us all the time, often begging● to be written, but we rarely take much notice of them. Stories seem to find me, rather than me consciously looking for one. My inspiration often comes from a real event.

What is the message in this story?
There are several messages in the story, but I think the most powerful one can be summed up● in the words of the English teacher in the film *Dead Poets Society* - "Seize● the day! Make your lives extraordinary!" We *can* change things. We *can* live the life we want and realize our full potential.

Have you any other stories planned for the future?
Yes, I have a file full of ideas for stories.

Glossary

- **begging:** (here) asking
- **finance:** get money for
- **graduation:** when you get a degree at a university
- **postgraduate:** detailed studies after a degree
- **seize:** take with force
- **summed up:** said in few words

Before Reading

1 The story *The Coconut Seller* takes place in Brazil.
How much do you know about Brazil? Do the quiz and find out.

a) Which city is the capital of Brazil?
1 ☐ Rio de Janeiro
2 ☐ Brasília
3 ☐ São Paulo

b) What is the estimated population of Brazil?
1 ☐ about 50 million
2 ☐ just over 100 million
3 ☐ nearly 200 million

c) Which is the largest city in Brazil?
1 ☐ São Paulo
2 ☐ Salvador
3 ☐ Rio de Janeiro

d) What is the official language in Brazil?
1 ☐ Spanish
2 ☐ French
3 ☐ Portuguese

e) Which country was Brazil a colony of?
1 ☐ Portugal
2 ☐ Great Britain
3 ☐ Spain

f) What is the name of the currency in Brazil?
1 ☐ dollar
2 ☐ real
3 ☐ peso

g) Brazil's large territory includes different ecosystems, such as ...
1 ☐ the Amazon Rainforest
2 ☐ the Great Barrier Reef
3 ☐ the Atacama Desert

h) What is the famous Sugarloaf in Brazil?
1 ☐ a typical sweet
2 ☐ a mountain in Rio de Janeiro
3 ☐ a popular beach in Bahia

i) Which of the following is NOT a famous beach in Rio de Janeiro.
1 ☐ Copacabana
2 ☐ Ipanema
3 ☐ Pantanal

j) What is samba?
1 ☐ a type of Brazilian dance and music genre
2 ☐ a typical Brazilian dish
3 ☐ a Brazilian festival

🎧 2 **Listen and check the answers.**

🗣 3 **With a partner write a quiz about another country you know or would like to visit. Then exchange your quiz with another pair.**

Before Reading

1 Check you know the meanings of the words below. They are all used in the story to describe three of the main characters: Bruno, Clara and Zeca. Put the words you think might refer to each of them in the column below each picture.

poor	tough	bad-tempered	optimistic	rich	menacing
enthusiastic	muscular	gorgeous	thug	hard-working	
fair-skinned	anxious	criminal	shy		

Bruno	Clara	Zeca

2 One of the three people above is the coconut seller. Who do you think it is? Who do you think are the hero and the villain in this story? Give reasons.

3 Look quickly at the cover of the book and the pictures inside. Then answer the questions.

a) What kind of story is it? Tick (✔).

☐ thriller / horror   ☐ adventure / drama
☐ science fiction   ☐ romantic comedy

b) What do you think happens in the story? Tick (✔) two items.

☐ a robbery   ☐ somebody is kidnapped
☐ a fatal accident   ☐ dreams comes true

4 In pairs choose a picture from the book and write a description. Then describe the picture to another pair. See if they can guess which picture it is.

5 Match the informal words and expressions from the book to their meanings.

a) ☐ rack one's brains   **1**   be cheerful and think of the positive aspects

b) ☐ look on the bright side   **2**   busy movement of a lot of people

c) ☐ hustle and bustle   **3**   go off in a noisy and angry way

d) ☐ picture in your mind's eye   **4**   I agree

e) ☐ seize the day   **5**   leave me alone

f) ☐ go figure   **6**   not what I like

g) ☐ give me a break   **7**   see in your imagination

h) ☐ storm off   **8**   take an opportunity as soon as it appears

i) ☐ it's a deal   **9**   tell you about

j) ☐ set in his ways   **10**   think a lot

k) ☐ not my scene   **11**   try to understand

l) ☐ fill you in on   **12**   who always does the same things

Before Reading

1 **How far do you agree with the following statements? Circle a score from 1 to 5 (1 = I totally disagree – 5 = I totally agree) for each one. Give your reasons and discuss with other students.**

a) We can change our lives. We can live the life we want.
   1   2   3   4   5

b) A movie or a book can really impress you and completely change your way of thinking.
   1   2   3   4   5

c) It is important to be polite to other people.
   1   2   3   4   5

d) It is better to be rich and unhappy than poor and happy.
   1   2   3   4   5

e) Parents should know everything about your lives.
   1   2   3   4   5

f) Sometimes you have to pretend to be something or someone you are not. You can't always be yourself.
   1   2   3   4   5

g) You should only go out with people of the same race or from the same background as yourself.
   1   2   3   4   5

h) Parents' opinions about the person you are going out with are very important.
   1   2   3   4   5

i) It's okay to bully people who are smaller or weaker than yourself.
   1   2   3   4   5

j) 'The end justifies the means.' This saying means that bad or unfair methods are acceptable if they allow you to achieve what you want, especially something good.
   1   2   3   4   5

2 Listen to these four extracts from the book and match each one to the chapter it was taken from.

Bruno

Bruno meets Clara

Bruno meets Clara's father

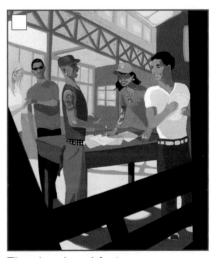

The abandoned factory

3 Choose one of the pictures above and imagine you are in the scene. Describe it in detail.

BRUNO

Bruno stopped what he was doing for a moment and sat down on a low wall in front of the beach. He stared out to sea with a broad* smile on his face, lost in thought as he enjoyed a moment's rest.

It was a hot, sultry* day like most summer days in Rio de Janeiro. It was only 11 o'clock in the morning and the temperature was already 35°C, and the humidity 82%. As usual, Bruno was wearing colourful, knee-length Bermuda shorts, a white sleeveless T-shirt, and a pair of blue flip-flops. The warm sea breeze* felt good against the smooth, dark skin of his face.

This was the day Bruno's life was going to change forever.

A group of girls walked past and smiled over at Bruno. He was slim and good-looking with short jet-black* hair and sparkling dark brown eyes. But Bruno wasn't just another good-looking guy*. He was one of life's genuine nice guys. He had a very distinctive, deep voice that was also pleasant and cheerful and warm. But he didn't use his voice to win people over*. No, whenever Bruno did say anything, it was always relevant and meaningful. His classmates at school teased him about being shy, but Bruno never got embarrassed or nervous; it was just the way he was. He kept himself to himself. And only spoke when he had something to say. Oh, and he had one of those irresistible smiles that light up your day. And he constantly looked on the bright side of things and was optimistic about everything. Quite simply, he was a nice happy guy and you couldn't help but like him.

Glossary
- **breeze:** light wind
- **broad:** (here) big
- **guy:** male
- **jet-black:** very black
- **sultry:** hot and heavy
- **win people over:** convince people of what he was saying

Bruno gazed• blankly at the hustle and bustle• on Ipanema• beach. The beach was crowded with rich, beautiful people, mainly Brazilians, but there were also lots of wealthy tourists, too. There were the usual sunworshippers• and surfers, and several groups of people playing football, volleyball and footvolley, a combination of volleyball and football which was invented in Brazil. Bruno looked to his right at the two mountains in the distance – the "Dois Irmãos" – the Two Brothers. Rio is such a beautiful place to live, he thought to himself.

BRAZIL

What do you know about Brazil?

Think, then share ideas with a partner.

What is your country famous for?
What tourist attractions are there?

Then he turned around and looked at all the sophisticated, high-rise• apartment buildings along the beach front. Ipanema was one of the best and most expensive places to live in Rio. But Bruno was really thinking of where *he* lived. Bruno lived in a favela, a kind of poor shanty• town, called Morro do Cantagalo, on the hill, behind these expensive flats.

Glossary

- **gazed:** looked in a fixed way
- **high-rise:** tall (of buildings); with many levels/floors
- **hustle and bustle:** busy movement
- **Ipanema:** rich neighbourhood in the south of Rio de Janeiro
- **shanty:** with poor, badly built houses and huts
- **sunworshippers:** people who love lying in the sun

In his mind's eye* he pictured the favela: hundreds of small, shabby*, randomly* built huts all crowded* close together on the hillside. He thought about the thousands of poor people living there, moving up and down along the complex network of stairways and tracks*, often on steep* inclines. The narrow winding* alleys* were too small and dangerous for cars and other vehicles.

The favela certainly wasn't an easy place to live and young people often turned to a life of crime. Bruno suddenly thought of Zeca. Zeca started stealing when he was only eight years old, now he was the neighbourhood tough guy*. Bruno hadn't seen him for years and he wasn't sorry. It's an unfair world we live in, Bruno thought. If you're poor you don't get much education and you've little chance of escaping from this situation. Bruno shivered and quickly thought of something more positive. He smiled as he thought of his mom and all the other ordinary people who lived in the favela, trying to earn an honest living. Day after day they walked up and down the steep steps into Rio to their low-paid, unskilled jobs. But they always had a smile and a big hello for everyone they met.

- **alleys:** narrow streets
- **crowded:** (here) built close together
- **mind's eye:** imagination
- **randomly:** not planned
- **shabby:** in bad condition
- **steep:** difficult to climb
- **tough guy:** bully
- **tracks:** paths
- **winding:** that turn round and round

When he was about eight years old Bruno asked his mother, "Why do we live here and not down there near the beach in those beautiful apartment blocks?"

"That's just the way things are, dear," his mother replied. "In this world there are rich people and there are poor people, and we are poor. There's no way we could ever live like them." He did not really understand this at that time.

Bruno then looked at the inside of his right forearm and the black tattoo he had recently got done there.

Carpe Diem was a quote from his favourite movie, *Dead Poets Society*. He'd seen the movie five years ago and it had had a profound effect on him. The story was about an English teacher, John Keating, in a school for boys. His lessons are unusual and unorthodox• and he inspires his students to change their lives and find the courage to do what they want in life. He tells them constantly, "Carpe diem. Seize• the day, boys! Make your lives extraordinary!"

Glossary

• **seize:** grab; take with your hands
• **unorthodox:** not usual or traditional

16

Yes! That's it! Bruno thought at the time. Things are not the way they are just because that's the way they are. We can change things. We *can* live the life we want!

What is your favourite movie?
Why? What is it about?

Have you ever seen a movie or read a book that has changed your way of thinking?

Do you think that we can change things and live the life we want?

Tell a partner.

Bruno decided there and then that he would not live the same life as his parents. He was determined to break away from the hardship• and poverty, and find a better life for himself and his family. He started to read as much as he possibly could, borrowing• books from the local library. He began studying really hard at school, too. And he did very well, getting high grades in all his subjects. But then two years ago, he had to leave school and go to work to help his family. That is when he got this job, selling coconuts at a small kiosk• on the beach front in Ipanema.

"Come on, Bruno, I have customers waiting!" his boss shouted, slightly annoyed that Bruno was still sitting on the wall.

"Okay, I'm coming!"

Bruno quickly stopped his daydreaming and jumped up. His break was over. It was time to get back to work.

- **borrowing:** taking something for a period of time
- **hardship:** economic difficulties

- **kiosk:** small open building (often selling newspapers or food)

BRUNO MEETS CLARA

The kiosk where Bruno worked was similar to all the other kiosks that dotted• the sidewalk• along Ipanema beach. It was a small, square-shaped shop, painted bright red, and conveniently placed between two palm trees that offered a bit of shade. There were a few plastic chairs and tables where customers could sit and chat with friends while they sipped• their coconut water.

When Bruno got back there the tables were full and there was a queue of people at the counter•. But he was a fast worker and pretty soon all the customers were served. He then went to get some more coconuts from the big refrigerator at the back of the kiosk.

"Hey, you! Give me a coconut water!" someone suddenly shouted rudely.

MANNERS

How do you think Bruno feels?
Has anyone ever been rude to you?
How did you react?

Bruno was facing the wall so he couldn't see who had spoken. Maybe I'll just pretend I didn't hear anything, he thought to himself. He moved his head to the side to sneak a look• at the rude customer. When he saw that it was a beautiful blonde girl he smiled to himself. Then he immediately walked over to the counter.

Glossary

- **counter:** flat surface in a shop or kiosk
- **dotted:** were spread about on
- **sidewalk:** (US) footpath; pavement
- **sipped:** drank slowly
- **sneak a look:** (here) look without her seeing him

"Good morning," Bruno said politely, as he smiled winningly* at the girl, revealing perfect, pearl-white* teeth. But she just ignored his greeting.

"Cut open a fresh coconut for me," she ordered, giving him a bad-tempered* scowl*.

"How much is it?" she continued brusquely* without even the slightest sign of a smile on her face.

Bruno served her in his usual efficient way.

She doesn't seem to be very happy. I wonder why. She's so gorgeous! he thought.

He found it odd* that so many of these rich young people who went to the kiosks did not seem to be particularly happy. His friends in the favela, who had lots to complain* about, were on the whole very cheerful and content. Go figure*! Bruno said to himself.

MONEY AND HAPPINESS

Think, then share ideas with a partner.

Do you need money to be happy?
Do you think money can buy you happiness?
What makes you happy? Write down three things.

Share with a partner.

The girl quickly drank her coconut water, paid and walked away without saying another word. Bruno kept silent, too, while she was there, and just got on* with his work. He watched her now as she

---

Glossary

- **bad-tempered:** angry
- **brusquely:** rudely
- **complain:** express discontent
- **go figure!:** (slang) try to understand
- **got on:** continued
- **odd:** strange
- **pearl-white:** very white
- **scowl:** unfriendly, angry expression
- **winningly:** in an attractive, charming way

crossed the road and went into one of the fancy* apartment buildings with huge verandas, facing the sea, right opposite the kiosk. I guess that's where she lives, Bruno thought. I wonder what it's like inside. Must be really cool!

"Where have you been, Clara? Wasting your time on the beach again, I'll bet!" her father commented as soon as she entered the living room.

"Hey, leave me alone, will you, dad?"

"You'll never get into university like that! You should be studying hard!"

"Oh, give me a break*!" Clara shouted back as she stormed off* into her room and slammed* the door behind her. Her father sighed* with despair*. He could never understand why Clara was always in such a bad mood. All he wanted was the best for his daughter, but he found it difficult to deal with* her, especially since her mother died.

MOODS

Do you ever get into bad moods?
When you are in a bad mood, do you treat everybody in the same way?
Are you especially hostile towards certain people? Who? Why?
How can you get out of a bad mood?

⯈ Make a list with a partner.

- **deal with:** handle and talk to
- **despair:** when you lose hope
- **fancy:** expensive
- **give me a break!:** (slang) leave me alone
- **sighed:** made a sad noise
- **slammed:** closed with a bang
- **stormed off:** went off in a noisy and angry way

Later that day, Bruno was on his own at the kiosk. He was leaning•
on the counter reading a book, waiting for customers. He was so
completely absorbed in his book that he did not notice when Clara
arrived. She looked at Bruno quizzically• for a moment.

"Oh, I'm sorry! I didn't see you there." Bruno quickly apologized
as he suddenly sensed that he was being looked at.

"It's OK, no problem", Clara muttered•.

"Are you really reading that book, *Captains of the Sand*? It's on the
syllabus• for the university entrance exams. I should be studying it,
but I hate reading. It's so boring. I'd much rather go to the beach or
the shopping mall•!"

"Hey, this book is really cool, you know!" Bruno replied
enthusiastically.

Glossary

- **leaning:** resting his body
- **mall:** lots of shops in one big centre
- **muttered:** said in a low voice
- **quizzically:** in a questioning way
- **syllabus:** list of things you must learn

"It's about a gang of orphans, from seven to fifteen years old – the captains of the sand. That's what they used to call abandoned street kids. They live in the streets of Salvador in Bahia, and the only way they can survive is by stealing. I'm reading it for the third time now."

"Yeah, right! Like you're an expert on Brazilian literature!" Clara retorted• disbelievingly. "Since when did a guy who sells coconut water waste• his time reading literature?"

"Well, do you want to know something? I love reading and I don't think it's a waste of time!"

"No way•! You're kidding• me, right?"

"No, I'm serious. I want to study Portuguese Language and Literature at university. So I'm studying now to pass the entrance exams for a public university. It's free there. My family's poor and I could never afford to go to a private university."

• **kidding:** joking
• **No way!:** (slang) that's not true!

• **retorted:** answered in a sharp way
• **waste:** use in a bad way

"Wow! That's amazing!" Clara said, finally convinced that Bruno was really telling the truth.

There was a brief, awkward silence. Bruno and Clara just looked at each other. Neither of them knew what to say next. Then Bruno broke the silence and asked, "So, what's your name?"

"I'm Clara. And you?"

"Bruno. Hey, Clara. If you want we could meet later and I could try to tell you why this book is so great. What do you think?"

"Hmm, I dunno•, my dad is very strict•. He doesn't let me stay out late. And I have to go to class later this afternoon. I'm doing one of those crash courses• for the university entrance exams. What time do you finish here?"

"Six o'clock."

"OK, I could meet you here at about six fifteen."

"Great! So I'll see you later then." Bruno said, beaming• with delight.

Clara turned round to walk away, when Bruno suddenly remembered something.

"Hey, Clara," he called after her. "I forgot to give you your coconut water!"

Clara smiled. "No problem! I forgot to ask for one!"

Clara arrived at the kiosk at six fifteen sharp•. Bruno had been waiting anxiously all afternoon. He wasn't sure that she would actually turn up•. They strolled• along the beach front, chatting about themselves. Then, as promised, Bruno told Clara about the book – *Captains of the Sand*. She listened, intrigued• and impressed•.

Glossary

- **beaming:** smiling
- **crash courses:** quick intensive courses
- **dunno:** don't know
- **impressed:** (she) understood it was important
- **intrigued:** interested
- **sharp:** (here) exactly
- **strict:** severe
- **strolled:** walked slowly
- **turn up:** appear

"This is amazing", Clara said. "You make it all sound so interesting. My Portuguese teacher at school is so boring. I wish I had a teacher like you. I've always found Portuguese really difficult, especially the literature. I'm good at math and I'm going to study architecture at university. I'm trying to get in to public university, too, as the courses are better. But the entrance exam is really difficult."

"Hey, why don't we give each other a hand? I'll help you with your Portuguese and you can help me with my math. I'm useless at math. So, what do you think?"

"OK, it's a deal•!"

Bruno held his hand out and said, "So, let's shake on it."

And they shook hands.

SCHOOL

What is your favourite subject at school?

What is your least favourite?

What would you like to do when you finish school?

Do you and your friends help each other like Bruno and Clara?

Bruno and Clara started meeting every day and pretty soon, as well as helping each other with their studies, they also started dating•. They were both very happy.

• **dating:** going out together

• **It's a deal!:** I agree!

Clara's dad, Pedro, was a tall, well-dressed, distinguished-looking man. He was fussy● and proud of his appearance. He was in his late forties● and his hair was starting to go grey at the sides. He was also beginning to lose his hair at the front. Once a month he had his hair cut at a madly expensive hairdressing salon, convinced that the more he paid, the less hair would fall out. He had green eyes and wore a pair of expensive glasses which he kept cleaning fastidiously● with a cotton handkerchief he always carried in his pocket.

Pedro's father had been an army officer. And although Pedro had never been in the army, he seemed to have inherited● his father's highly organized and methodical way of doing everything. He was also very set in his ways●, with deeply-rooted● habits and very strong opinions, often refusing to even consider what other people thought.

APPEARANCES

Are you fussy about your appearance?
How long does it take you to get ready before you go out?
Describe your appearance to a partner.

Glossary

- **deeply-rooted:** that are there for a long time
- **fastidiously:** carefully (in an exaggerated way)
- **fussy:** paying great attention to detail
- **inherited:** got something from someone else
- **late forties:** 48 or 49 years old
- **set in his ways:** who always has the same ideas and does the same things

Pedro was an only son and had inherited from his father the family furniture-making business. He was rich and successful but had few real friends. His wife, Clara's mother, had been his only real friend, and when she died of cancer three years ago, Pedro was devastated•.

After her death he decided to move to the apartment in Ipanema with his only daughter, Clara. He could no longer bear to stay in the house where they had all lived together. There were too many memories there and he wanted to make a new start in life.

Pedro arrived home from work one day, and while he was waiting for the elevator•, the concierge• of the building came up to him, smiled politely and said, "Good evening, Senhor Pedro. I see your daughter's dating now. He looks like a nice, hard-working, young man. You must be happy."

But Pedro wasn't happy. He just nodded•. The elevator arrived and the concierge held the door open for him. Pedro marched into the elevator, seething with anger•.

• **concierge:** porter in a building or hotel
• **devastated:** destroyed
• **elevator:** (US) lift

• **nodded:** moved his head up and down to say 'yes'
• **seething with anger:** very angry

"Clara!" he shouted as soon as he walked into the apartment. "Where are you?"

"I'm here, dad! Calm down!"

When Clara saw her father's bright red face she knew it was something serious.

"What's the matter, dad?"

"Just answer my question! Are you going out with some guy that I've never even heard about?" he shouted.

"Yes!" replied Clara, firmly•. "What's the big deal•? I'm not a little kid any more! I'm seventeen years old, dad!"

"Yes, and old enough to get into trouble. You're still my daughter and you do what I tell you, young lady. Don't forget that!"

PARENTS

What type of relationship does Clara have with her father?
How do you get on• with your parents?
Do you tell them everything?
Who makes the rules in your house?

"Come on, dad," Clara sighed in exasperation•. She felt a bit calmer now after her little outburst•.

"Bruno is a really nice guy, and I like him – a lot!"

Glossary

- **exasperation:** frustration (when you don't know what to do next)
- **firmly:** in a sure, strong way
- **how do you get on:** what is your relationship like
- **outburst:** sudden expression of anger
- **What's the big deal?:** What's the problem?

"So, who is this Bruno guy anyway?" her father asked sternly•. He had calmed down, too.

Clara told her dad that she had met Bruno at the kiosk and that he was helping her with her studies so that she could pass the university entrance exams. She didn't mention• that Bruno worked at the kiosk and that he lived in the favela. She also confessed to him that the relationship was getting serious.

Pedro listened carefully, then said, "I want to meet him. I'll book a table for the three of us at that nice Italian restaurant on the corner, for eight o'clock tomorrow night. And tell him not to be late. You know how I hate having to wait for people."

• **mention:** say

• **sternly:** in a serious and cross way

Bruno felt a moment of sheer• panic when Clara told him that
her father wanted to meet him at the restaurant. I don't even have
a shirt or tie! he thought. And I can't possibly turn up in shorts and
a T-shirt. Then he thought of Tiago, his neighbour. Tiago always
wore a shirt and tie for special occasions and he was about the same
size as Bruno. Tiago was only too happy to help Bruno out. He even
knotted• the tie for him. Bruno had never worn a tie before.

"How can you wear this thing?" Bruno asked his friend, pulling at
the collar of his shirt to loosen his tie.

"You'll get used to it," his friend said, laughing. "Now stop
messing about with the collar."

Glossary

• **knotted:** tied

• **sheer:** (here) complete

30

Bruno's mother came into the room and stood there for a moment, gazing lovingly at her son.

"Goodness gracious! What a handsome young man we have here!"

"Thanks mom. I feel so nervous. I really want Clara's dad to like me."

"How could he possibly not like you? Just mind* your manners* and don't pretend to be someone you're not. Be yourself. That's who Clara fell for* in the first place, isn't it?" And she gave a chuckle* of delight.

PRETENDING

What does Bruno's mother mean when she says: "don't pretend to be someone you're not"?

Have you ever pretended to be different from the way you are?

Are you the same with everybody that you know?

"Now off you go and enjoy yourself!" she said, giving him a big hug and a kiss. Bruno rushed out of the room, worried that he might be late.

At five minutes to eight, Bruno was standing outside the restaurant. He had never been anywhere like this before in his life. Beads* of sweat started to roll down his face as he stood petrified between two large marble pillars, staring at the door. Then he took a couple of deep breaths. Okay, here we go, he said to himself and he opened the main door.

- **beads:** little drops
- **chuckle:** little laugh
- **fell for:** fell in love with
- **manners:** how you act/behave
- **mind:** be careful of

His confidence quickly disappeared as soon as he entered the restaurant. He had never seen a place like this before. There were big, sparkling chandeliers• hanging from the ceiling and plush•, deep-pile• carpets on the floor. The round tables all had white linen tablecloths and the comfortable, padded chairs were upholstered• in deep red satin. Bruno stared at the bewildering• array• of knives, forks, spoons, plates and glasses on each of the tables.

"Oh, boy, this is not going to be easy!" he thought to himself.

Then he saw Clara rushing towards him. What a relief!

"Hiya! I'm not late, am I?" he asked, as he kissed her quickly on the cheek. He was afraid her dad might not want him to kiss her on the lips.

"No, you're right on time. Come on. My dad's over there, waiting to meet you." She took his hand and led him over to the table, where Pedro was sitting. Pedro stood up, politely introduced himself, and then quickly said, "I've already ordered for all of us. I presume• you like your pasta *al dente*•?"

"Yes, of course," Bruno answered, not having the slightest idea what *al dente* was, but since it had already been ordered, it did not make any difference.

The atmosphere was tense and strained• and Bruno was feeling very uncomfortable with the whole situation.

UNCOMFORTABLE SITUATIONS

Have you ever been in an uncomfortable situation?

Describe it to a partner.

What did you do?

Glossary

- **al dente:** way of cooking pasta (so it is not too soft)
- **array:** selection
- **bewildering:** confusing
- **chandeliers:** large glass lamps that hang from the ceiling
- **deep-pile:** thick (of carpets)
- **plush:** soft and luxurious
- **presume:** imagine to be true
- **strained:** tense; not relaxed
- **upholstered:** covered (of furniture)

Pedro was very pleasant at first, but soon the polite conversation turned to more straightforward questions about Bruno's family and his plans for the future.

"What kind of future are you going to offer my daughter?" Pedro asked bluntly•.

Before Bruno could reply, a middle-aged• couple approached their table, calling out, "Pedro, fancy• seeing you here! How are you?"

Pedro jumped up with a big smile on his face: it was one of his best customers with his wife. Even though they were not invited, they quickly sat down at Pedro's table and were briefly introduced to Clara and Bruno.

The tense atmosphere immediately became more relaxed. Even Pedro was more talkative and friendly.

Then Carlos, Pedro's customer, smiled at Bruno and asked, "So what do you do, Bruno?"

"I work." Bruno replied, shifting• about uneasily• on his chair.

"What kind of work?"

"Sales," he continued, not knowing quite what to say.

"A kiosk." Clara chipped in•, trying to help the conversation run more smoothly.

"Ah, you own a kiosk! Very nice! I believe there's a lot of easy profit there."

"No, I sell coconut water at a kiosk on the beach front," Bruno added.

There was a sudden silence and it felt so tense that you could have cut the air with a knife. Then, in an instant the bill was paid and they all rapidly went their separate ways.

Glossary

- **bluntly:** in a direct way
- **chipped in:** said; added (to a conversation)
- **fancy:** (here) imagine
- **middle-aged:** 45-60 years old
- **shifting:** (here) moving
- **uneasily:** in a nervous way

After that evening, Pedro was convinced that Bruno was not good enough for his daughter, and made it quite clear to her that he was totally against the idea of her dating a mixed-race guy from a completely different background. He told her to stop seeing Bruno and made her stay at home in the evenings to study, on her own.

BRUNO AND CLARA

Do you think Clara's dad is fair?

Do you think parents should decide who their children date?

Can you think of any other stories like Bruno and Clara's, where parents tried to stop their children from seeing each other?

Clara, of course, continued to meet Bruno secretly during the day time. And every evening before returning to the favela after work, Bruno waited under her balcony so that she could blow kisses down to him and wave goodbye.

Clara had never been to visit Bruno's family in the favela. Her father always kept a close eye on her, especially after that unforgettable dinner at the restaurant. Bruno had invited her many times, and she really wanted to meet his family, specially his mother. She really admired Bruno's mother for bringing up* three children on her own, as a poor, single mother.

Then one day, unexpectedly, Pedro announced that he had to go to São Paulo for work for the weekend for a furniture exhibition. He was worried about Clara but she said she would stay with a friend and study. She didn't say that she'd go to Bruno's house, too.

Bruno was delighted when Clara told him that she was going to visit them. He told his mother immediately and she said she would cook one of her famous *feijoadas*. Dona Maria's *feijoada* was said to be the best in the favela, and, probably, in the whole of Brazil.

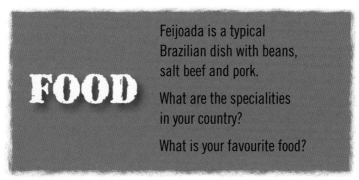

FOOD

Feijoada is a typical Brazilian dish with beans, salt beef and pork.

What are the specialities in your country?

What is your favourite food?

Bruno picked Clara up in front of her apartment on Saturday morning and they took a bus to the bottom of the hill where the favela was located. Then they started the long climb up the steep, winding steps. Clara had tried to prepare herself before coming, but everyone seemed to be even poorer than she had imagined.

Glossary

• **bringing up:** looking after children as they grow up

As soon as they entered Bruno's house, Dona Maria rushed over to them and threw her arms around Clara, kissing her on both cheeks.

"Welcome to my home, Clara. I'm so happy to meet you. Bruno has told us all about you. Please make yourself at home. It's all very simple here, but you won't go hungry. I'm making my special *feijoada*. And it's nearly ready."

"Thanks, Dona Maria, it's really great to be here and to meet you," Clara said, still a little overwhelmed° by everything. Bruno led° her into the living room where she met his younger brother and sister and lots of other relatives and friends who had come as usual for their Saturday lunch. Everyone welcomed Clara with open arms and the atmosphere was so relaxed and friendly that she soon felt as if she had known them all her life.

• **led:** guided; showed her the way

• **overwhelmed:** feeling too much emotion

After lunch everyone moved to the flat, open roof of the house. Musical instruments suddenly appeared from nowhere. Soon everyone was either playing, singing or dancing to the beat• of the samba. There were all kinds of drums, and stringed instruments, tambourines, shakers, scrapers, and bells. Bruno picked up a *cuíca*, a drum that makes a high-pitched• squeaky• noise. Clara laughed in delight and tapped• her feet to the rhythm.

"I feel so stupid! I don't know how to play anything," she whispered into Bruno's ear, feeling left out.

"Of course you do," Bruno said, laughing. "Here you are!" And he gave her a whistle. "Just blow it when you feel like it. You can't go wrong!"

They played, sang and danced the whole afternoon and into the early hours of the evening. Clara couldn't remember the last time that she had enjoyed herself so much.

MUSIC

What is your favourite type of music?

Who are your favourite singers and bands?

Can you play an instrument? Which one?

Would you like to be able to play an instrument? Which one?

Glossary

- **beat:** rhythm; musical sound
- **high-pitched:** that makes a high sound
- **squeaky:** high sound
- **tapped:** moved (feet or hands) to follow a rhythm/musical sound

Clara had often heard about the *baile funk* dance parties that took place in the favelas, but she had never been to one herself. This was her chance to finally go to one, so she asked Bruno if he would take her that evening. She had listened to some of the music at home: funky* rhythms with strong rap-style lyrics often about important social issues* such as poverty, racism, violence and justice. As they walked towards the dance hall, she felt excited yet also a bit anxious and on edge*. Her father would go mad if he ever found out where she was going.

RAP The word rap is an acronym*.

What do the letters R A P stand for?
Do you like rap?
What famous rappers do you know?
Do you think music can change society? How?

With a partner think of songs that have strongly influenced the way people think and act.

When they arrived, the huge dance hall was already packed to capacity* with hundreds of young people from the favela. The music was deafeningly* loud, and people were dancing like crazy everywhere. Clara felt like a fish out of water. Bruno put his arm around her and held her close to him the whole time, which made her feel warm and protected. After a while, she turned to Bruno and said, "Shall we go? I feel a bit uncomfortable. This really isn't my scene*. Do you mind?"

Glossary

- **acronym:** word formed by initial letters of other words
- **deafeningly:** so loud it made you deaf (that you cannot hear)
- **funky:** music rhythm that mixes jazz and blues

- **issues:** questions
- **my scene:** (slang) what I like
- **on edge:** not relaxed; nervous
- **packed to capacity:** completely full of people

"Of course not," Bruno said, smiling. "It's not my thing*, either. I didn't think you'd really like it. I just need to go to the bathroom. Stay here and don't move. I'll be right back, OK?"

Clara watched Bruno as he disappeared into the crowd. Soon he was completely out of sight. A split second* later, a tall heavy-set* man appeared in front of her. He was wearing a tight white T-shirt that showed off his muscular arms.

"What does the bouncer* want with me?" Clara thought to herself as she moved away from him. But the man stepped forward. He was standing so close to her that she could feel his hot, smelly breath on her face.

"Hey, babe! What's a pretty little rich girl like you doing here?"

Clara's heart pounded* with fear and she wished with all her heart that Bruno would come back quickly.

FEAR

Clara is afraid. Imagine you are in her situation. What would you do? Think of a time when you felt afraid. What happened? What did you do?

Make a list of the things you are afraid of. Share with a partner.

"I'm with my boyfriend. He's just gone to the bathroom. He'll be right back any second now." Clara sounded sure of herself but she felt like crying.

The man put his arm around Clara's shoulders. "Aw, come on. Let's have a dance while you're waiting for him," the man insisted with a sleazy* smile. But just then Bruno came running towards him.

- **bouncer:** someone who throws people out of a night club, etc.
- **heavy-set:** robust; broad and muscular
- **not my thing:** not something I like

- **pounded:** beat; made regular loud sounds
- **sleazy:** dishonest and with bad intentions
- **split second:** one second; very soon

"Get your hands off her, Zeca!" Bruno shouted.

Then Bruno suddenly felt a sharp pain in both sides of his head as two guns were pressed violently against his ears by the big guy's bodyguards. Bruno froze•, paralyzed with fear.

"It's OK!" the man shouted, laughing loudly. "Let him go. He's my friend. Right, Bruno? Hey, man, long time no see, eh? So what's up? I see you've got yourself a nice lady!"

"All's well, man." Bruno replied.

After a few seconds of strained silence, Bruno added, "We've got to go now, OK? So, see you around, right?"

"Yeah, see you, man. You take care now," Zeca said, nodding his head, with a menacing• look.

Bruno took a deep breath and gave Clara an apologetic smile. She was shaking with fear. Bruno took her by the hand and they slowly walked away in silence, not daring• to look back.

Bruno had a terrible sinking feeling in the pit of his stomach•. He knew that he would be seeing Zeca again very soon.

Glossary

- **froze:** stopped moving
- **daring:** (here) having the courage
- **menacing:** threatening; that made others afraid
- **sinking ... stomach:** bad feeling about what is going to happen

ZECA'S EVIL PLAN

José Carlos dos Santos had been given the nickname Zeca when he was just a kid, and it had stuck•. He was always much bigger and stronger than the other boys of his age and he often bullied anyone who was smaller and weaker than he was. Soon all the children in the neighbourhood were afraid of him, and what Zeca said, ruled•.

Have you ever been bullied?
Do you know any bullies?

BULLYING

With a partner think of ways to stop bullying.

Now that Zeca had grown up he was head and shoulders above everyone else in the area. And he made sure he was stronger, too, spending his afternoons pumping iron• at the local gym. Big, tall and muscular: nobody messed• with Zeca.

Zeca had learned to look after himself at an early age. When he was just eight years old, his father was sent to prison for stealing cars. His mother was hardly ever at home and Zeca had to survive on his own. He soon turned to• petty crime•, which quickly escalated into more serious offences such as mugging• and extortion•. He was a tough kid and by the age of eighteen he had his own gang of thugs• and hoodlums•.

- **extortion:** forcing people to give you money
- **hoodlums:** tough guys
- **messed:** (here) interfered
- **mugging:** attacking people
- **petty crime:** small illegal actions
- **pumping iron:** weightlifting; using the weights at the gym
- **ruled:** was law
- **stuck:** (here) stayed
- **thugs:** criminals
- **turned to:** started doing

Zeca put his first gang of thieves together in the favela when he was only thirteen years old. He and his gang also controlled the games of football the boys used to play on a small piece of open land in the favela. At that time, Bruno was ten and he often went to watch the older boys play. Everyone dreamed of becoming a famous footballer like Adriano, and getting out of the favela forever.

One day, Zeca's team was a player short•. He looked closely and intently for a few moments at all the young spectators, who were sitting on the walls around the playing field, waiting for the game to start. Then he fixed his gaze• on Bruno and called out, "So, do you want to play or what?"

"Me?" Bruno asked in amazement. He went numb•. He could not believe his ears.

Glossary

• **a player short:** with one less player
• **gaze:** look

• **numb:** when you can't feel anything

44

"Who do you think I'm talking to?" Zeca shouted, starting to get a bit angry.

Bruno jumped up and ran onto the football pitch•, filled with excitement.

It was a difficult game, and at the end of the first half, Zeca's team were losing 1-0. Bruno had been playing in the fullback position. Just before the second half started, Zeca called Bruno over and said, "I'm going to move you up front. Let's see how good you are." Then he continued threateningly "You'd better score at least two goals. My team never loses. Got it?"

Bruno was terrified, but as soon as the game started again, he forgot about Zeca and focused on winning. He played brilliantly and scored two spectacular goals. Another boy from his team also scored, making the final score 3-1. They had won!

• **pitch:** sports field

"You're cool, man!" Zeca said to him after the game. "You can come and play for us whenever you want, OK?"

"Thanks, Zeca," Bruno replied, knowing deep inside that this would not be a good idea. After winning the football game, Bruno also won Zeca's protection in the favela and nobody dared* to mess with him. Bruno was grateful* for this, but Zeca also wanted him to join his gang of criminals, and this was something Bruno definitely did not want.

For a couple of years after this first game, Bruno used to play the odd* game of football just to keep in Zeca's good books*. He hadn't played a game or seen Zeca for two years, since he started working at the coconut kiosk. Until now. The chance meeting with Zeca at the dance party had left Bruno worried. He knew it was only a matter of time* before Zeca would appear again.

Zeca showed up* sooner than Bruno had expected. About a week after the dance party, he was coming home from work when two men suddenly stepped out of an alleyway* and pushed him up against the wall. They grabbed* him by the arms and one of them said, "Zeca wants to see you, now! Come with us."

They dragged* him through several streets, and then pushed him down some steps and into a nearby house. Zeca was already there waiting for him. He was sitting on a high stool, whistling to himself.

"Hey, Bruno! How nice of you to come and visit your old friend," he said, smirking* sarcastically. "Sit down. You and I have some serious things to talk about."

Glossary

- **alleyway:** dark narrow street
- **dared:** tried (to do something difficult or foolish)
- **dragged:** pulled along the ground
- **grabbed:** took with force
- **grateful:** thankful
- **keep... books:** stay in his favour/that he likes him
- **matter of time:** a short time
- **odd:** occasional; not very often
- **showed up:** appeared
- **smirking:** smiling unpleasantly

Zeca then told him all about a foolproof° plan he had to steal the official university entrance exams, and sell them before the day of the exam. He had a contact at the company where the exams were printed and he was going to make a copy of the papers for Zeca.

"Now this is where you come in°," he continued to explain. "You and that pretty little rich girlfriend of yours are going to help us sell the results to her friends, all those rich kids in Ipanema. And I'll give you and the girl the papers, too. So you both get into university. That's what you always wanted, isn't it, Bruno?"

BRUNO

What do you think Bruno is going to do?

What would you do?

What advice would you give Bruno?

Bruno sat, speechless°. He was in a state of total shock. Before he could collect himself°, Zeca went on, "Oh, and by the way, just in case you're thinking about pulling a fast one° and not helping us, we know where Clara and her dad live. We can pay them a surprise visit any time we want. And I don't think they'd be too happy to see us."

Zeca cackled° with laughter while Bruno was led outside, as white as a sheet.

- **cackled:** laughed unpleasantly
- **collect himself:** become calm again
- **come in:** (here) are needed
- **foolproof:** that cannot fail
- **pulling a fast one:** (slang) doing something to trick Zeca
- **speechless:** without speaking

Bruno was now facing a real dilemma•.

On the one hand, he now had a quick way to escape from his dead-end• life in the favela. If he helped Zeca to sell the stolen exam results he had a guarantee of a free place at one of the top universities. A sure passport to a better future, and the fast track• to wealth and maybe even happiness.

On the other hand, Zeca was asking him to do something illegal and bad. A society needs rules and systems, Bruno thought. If you break the rules and cheat the systems, it's wrong, morally wrong.

Bruno's mother had always tried to teach him the difference between right and wrong, and the importance of keeping on the right side of the law.

But if I don't do what Zeca wants, I'll be putting the lives of Clara and her father seriously at risk, Bruno thought.

Bruno didn't know what to do, torn between doing the right thing and going for the quick fix to his difficult life.

RIGHT AND WRONG

Imagine you are in Bruno's situation. What would you do?

Is there any time when it is possible to justify doing something wrong? If so, when?

Bruno racked his brains• for ways to escape from his predicament•. Then he finally decided what to do.

Glossary

- **dead-end:** (here) without hope for the future
- **dilemma:** difficult choice
- **predicament:** difficult situation
- **racked his brains:** thought a lot
- **track:** way

He had not told Clara yet about his meeting with Zeca. He knew she would be terrified. But now it was time to tell her everything that had happened, and explain to her what he was going to do. They met in front of Clara's apartment building. And slowly Bruno told her everything. Then he phoned Zeca.

"OK, Zeca, we'll do it. But first you must promise me that Clara and her dad won't get hurt."

"No problem. You have my word. It's time to get moving, Bruno! Come to my place right away. The rest of the gang will be there, too. We'll fill you in on° all the details." Then Zeca gave Bruno directions to a store° on one of the street corners in the favela. One of Zeca's men would meet him there and take him to the gang's hideout°.

Sure enough a tall, vicious-looking man was waiting for him. He led Bruno along narrow, winding tracks, up to the highest spot on the hill.

The midday sun was blazing down and Bruno felt he was being watched for the whole journey. He took off his sunglasses to wipe his brow with a handkerchief, but he put them back on again when he saw Zeca and his gang come into sight. They were sitting round a big table in the backyard of a house, playing cards.

"Hey, Bruno! Great to see you, man!" Zeca shouted. "Come over here and meet the boys."

But before Bruno could move he was frisked° by two guards. He cringed° as the men searched his body for hidden guns, knives or other weapons°.

"He's clean, boss," one of the men shouted out.

- **cringed:** made an expression of embarrassment
- **fill you in on:** tell you about
- **frisked:** searched his body
- **hideout:** place where people hide
- **store:** shop
- **weapons:** arms; instruments like guns or knives to hurt people

Zeca introduced all the members of his gang, including the man who worked inside the printer's who was going to steal the exams. He then explained all the details of the plan. It seemed foolproof. There was no way anything could go wrong.

They all shook hands and quickly left.

Bruno's heart was beating fast. He was anxious to get away from the gang and phone Clara. He raced down the hill. Then he stopped at the bottom and looked behind him. It was clear, no one was following him. He took out his phone and called Clara.

"Hey, Clara. Listen." He was out of breath, panting heavily. "Everything went according to plan. To my plan, of course, not Zeca's!" he added, laughing excitedly.

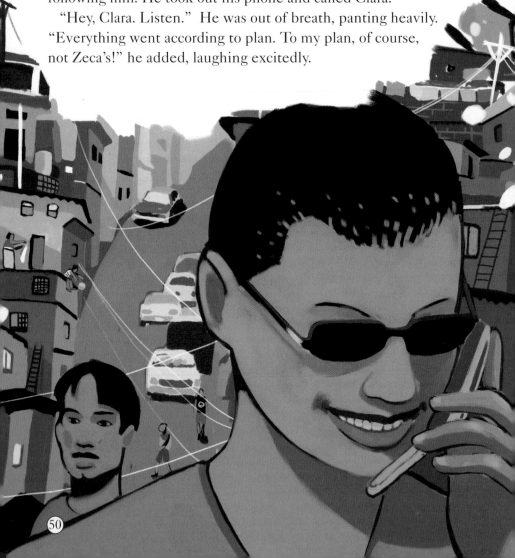

THE ABANDONED FACTORY

"This is amazing!" the police officer said, smiling broadly, as he looked at Bruno and Clara, who were sitting in front of him at the police station. "Well done! How did you manage to come up with such a brilliant idea?"

"Thanks. I guess it was kind of clever." Bruno answered, acknowledging• the compliment• with a polite smile. He felt slightly embarrassed. "Believe it or not, the idea just popped into my head while I was taking a shower. I remembered I saw an advert once on the Internet for special spy-camera sunglasses. They have a tiny, hidden, built-in• video recorder. Here they're only used by detectives and law enforcement agencies•, but anybody can buy them on the Internet."

When Bruno talked to Clara before his meeting with Zeca's gang, they both agreed it would be wrong to steal the exams, and help Zeca sell them to other people. But Bruno had worked out an ingenious plan to double-cross• Zeca and stay out of trouble himself.

First of all, he had wisely agreed to go along with• Zeca's plan, and go to the meeting with the gang of thieves. When he arrived at the hideout, they frisked him for hidden weapons, but no one ever imagined that Bruno was wearing sunglasses with a tiny built-in camera. Bruno had secretly videoed the entire meeting, making sure he had taken close-up• shots• of all the gang members. Their conversations with all the details of their plan had also been recorded.

Glossary

- **acknowledging:** recognising
- **built-in:** that is part of another structure
- **close-up:** from a close distance
- **compliment:** nice comment about someone
- **double-cross:** trick someone without them knowing
- **go along with:** agree to
- **law enforcement agencies:** police
- **shots:** (here) photographs

Then, as soon as he was sure that he wasn't being followed, he phoned Clara and together they went to the police with the camera and told them the whole story.

"Thanks to this evidence we can finally catch Zeca and his entire gang red-handed•," the police officer continued. "But we need you and Clara to help us. It's very important that you both continue to act as if nothing has happened. You must play along• with whatever Zeca wants. We'll be following your every move• from now on. Just do everything Zeca tells you to, OK?"

The police then went to the printer's and spoke to the owner. He agreed to co-operate and they installed some hidden cameras there, too. The day of the theft they saw the thief copy the exam papers on CCTV•, but they did not arrest him yet.

Then they waited until Zeca made the next move.

Two days later, Bruno was working as usual at the kiosk when his phone rang. It was Zeca. Zeca told him to go with Clara to an old abandoned factory several miles outside of town. The exam papers were ready. Bruno then called Clara and told her to meet him as soon as possible at the kiosk, so that they could go together. Then he phoned the police to give them the details.

When Bruno and Clara arrived, all the members of the gang were already there waiting for them. They were all laughing and joking, celebrating the success of the theft. Bruno and Clara joined them and started opening the packets to have a look at the stolen exam papers.

Glossary

- **CCTV:** security camera
- **move:** action
- **play along:** agree; pretend everything is fine

- **red-handed:** in the act of doing something wrong

Suddenly the doors crashed open and a loud, firm voice cried out, "Police! Drop your guns! Get down on your knees with your hands above your heads!"

No one heard what was said next as there was a sudden burst of gunfire. People were running all over the place, and clouds of dust flew up from the dirty, old floorboards.

Suddenly a raucous voice yelled out several times, "Hold your fire!" Everyone fell silent. The dust started to settle. Zeca was standing in the middle of the room holding a gun to Clara's head. He screamed out wildly, "Put your guns down and kick them over here! Now lie on the floor – everybody! Or she's dead!"

The police threw down their guns and kicked them towards Zeca. One of the guns bounced across the floor and landed• right in front of Bruno, who was kneeling on the floor behind Zeca. Bruno had no time to think. Almost instinctively he grabbed the gun, aimed• it at Zeca's legs and fired. Zeca dropped to the ground. Clara ran towards Bruno.

More armed policemen came rushing in and quickly took control of the situation. Zeca and the rest of the gang were quickly handcuffed• and led off to the police cars waiting outside.

Clara fell into Bruno's arms crying and shaking. Neither of them spoke a word. They were both in a state of shock.

COURAGE

Think of a time when you showed courage.
Tell a partner what happened and what you did.

Glossary

- **aimed:** pointed
- **landed:** fell to the ground
- **handcuffed:** put metal handcuffs on

EPILOGUE

🎧 One month later.

Soon after the police raid•, Bruno and Clara took the university entrance exams. They both passed and got into the top university. The authorities were very grateful to Bruno and Clara for stopping the theft and sale of the exams. As well as a full scholarship•, they both received a very generous grant• from the government to cover all their living expenses for the four years of their courses.

On Saturday, Clara's dad, Pedro, organized a celebration lunch at his apartment. Bruno was standing alone on the balcony, gazing out to sea, when Pedro came and stood beside him.

He smiled nervously at Bruno and said, "Look Bruno, I really want to apologize. When I first met you, I thought you weren't good enough for my daughter. But now I can assure you that I'm glad you had the courage to follow your heart. You saved her life! I can never repay you for that. Please forgive me." Pedro looked at Bruno with tears welling• in his eyes.

FORGIVENESS

If you were Bruno, would you forgive Pedro?
Think of a time when you forgave someone.
Now think of a time when someone forgave you.

• **grant:** money given to student
• **raid:** surprise attack

• **scholarship:** payment for a course
• **welling:** filling

"Of course I forgive you." Bruno said, smiling warmly. "It was a difficult time for all of us, but all's well that ends well, right?"

They hugged each other without saying anything. Then Bruno broke the silence.

"I wonder if lunch is ready," he said. "I'm starving!"

Then a happy, singsong voice called out from the kitchen.

"Come on everybody!" Dona Maria proudly announced.

"You know something, Bruno." Pedro said in a loud voce. "Your mom's *feijoada* beats pasta al dente any day!"

They all burst out laughing as they rushed into the dining room.

After Reading

Personal Response

1 Did you like the story? Why/why not?

2 Could this story take place in your country? If not, why not?

3 Which part of the story did you enjoy most? Explain why.

4 What did you think about Bruno's plan? Would you do the same in his situation?

5 Is there anything you would like to change in the story? Give details.

6 Do you think there are any messages in this story? What are they?

7 Did you like the ending of the story? Did you find it surprising? What did you think would happen?

8 Suggest other ways in which the story could end.

9 Imagine you are making a film of the story. Which famous actors would you choose to play the major roles? What theme song or music would you choose for the film?

After Reading

Comprehension

1 Tick (✔) T (true), F (false) or D (doesn't say).

	T	F	D
a) Bruno is the owner of a kiosk in Ipanema.	☐	☐	☐
b) Bruno really likes Brazilian literature.	☐	☐	☐
c) Clara had a rich boyfriend before she met Bruno.	☐	☐	☐
d) Clara's mother died suddenly and unexpectedly of cancer.	☐	☐	☐
e) Clara's dad, Pedro, meets Bruno for the first time at an Italian restaurant.	☐	☐	☐
f) Bruno always wears a collar and tie.	☐	☐	☐
g) Dona Maria, Bruno's mother, makes Clara feel really welcome when she visits their home in the favela.	☐	☐	☐
h) Zeca only thought of stealing the exams after he met Bruno and Clara at the dance hall.	☐	☐	☐
i) Bruno has played football regularly for Zeca's team since he was 12 years old.	☐	☐	☐
j) Bruno agrees to take part in Zeca's plan, but he does not really intend to help him sell the stolen exams.	☐	☐	☐
k) Zeca is shot and dies during the police raid.	☐	☐	☐
l) Bruno and Clara get married before they start their university course.	☐	☐	☐

2 Answer the questions.

a) Why did Bruno have the tattoo *Carpe Diem* on his right forearm?

b) Why was Clara so happy when her father had to travel to São Paulo to go to an exhibition?

c) Why did Bruno agree at first to go along with Zeca's scheme? What did he really plan to do?

3 Write a 150-word summary of the story, but deliberately include 3 incorrect pieces of information. Exchange with a partner and try to discover the mistakes.

4 Write a 150-word summary, but with the sentences mixed up or cut up on separate pieces of paper. Exchange with a partner and try to put the sentences in the correct order.

5 In pairs, write three questions about the story. Then exchange with another pair and answer each other's questions.

6 Match the first part of the sentence from the story to the second part.

a) ☐ This was the day Bruno's life

b) ☐ We can live

c) ☐ Just mind

d) ☐ Bruno was feeling very uncomfortable

e) ☐ What kind of future are you going

f) ☐ It's all very simple here,

g) ☐ How nice of you to come

h) ☐ You and I have some serious things

i) ☐ Put your guns down

j) ☐ I'm glad you had the courage

1 to offer my daughter?

2 with the whole situation.

3 to talk about.

4 the life we want.

5 was going to change forever.

6 to follow your heart.

7 and kick them over here.

8 but you won't go hungry.

9 and visit your old friend.

10 your manners.

7 When did the sentences occur in the story? Discuss with a partner.

After Reading

Characters

1 Who is speaking? Who are they talking to? What is the situation?

a) Yeah, right! Like you're an expert on Brazilian literature.

.... ➡ ....

b) Get your hands off her!

.... ➡ ....

c) That's just the way things are, dear. In this world there are rich people and there are poor people, and we are poor.

.... ➡ ....

d) I feel so stupid! I don't know how to play anything.

.... ➡ ....

e) You'd better score at least two goals. My team never loses. Got it?

.... ➡ ....

f) If you want we could meet later and I could try to tell you why this book is so great.

.... ➡ ....

g) You saved her life. I can never repay you for that. Please forgive me.

.... ➡ ....

h) What's a pretty little rich girl like you doing here?

.... ➡ ....

i) Are you going out with some guy I've never even heard about?

.... ➡ ....

j) Everything went according to plan. To my plan, of course, not Zeca's!

.... ➡ ....

2 The words and phrases below are used in the story to describe four characters. Put them in the correct columns. One is used twice.

heavy-set	dark brown eyes	blonde hair	big	tall	young

jet-black hair   hair turning grey at the sides   beautiful   muscular

good-looking   well-dressed   smelly breath   fair-skinned   slim

gorgeous   distinguished-looking   in his late forties   cheerful

Bruno	Clara	Zeca	Pedro

3 Who is your favourite character? Explain why.

4 Find examples of words or actions in the story that illustrate the following. Discuss them with your partner.

a) Clara is hostile towards her father and argues with him.

b) Bruno is brave.

c) Clara's father is concerned about his daughter's welfare.

d) Bruno's mother is kind and loving.

e) Zeca is cruel and threatening.

f) Bruno is enthusiastic and hard-working.

g) Clara's father worries too much about details and standards.

h) Bruno is honest.

i) Zeca is the leader of a criminal gang.

j) Bruno's mother is a good cook.

After Reading

Plot and Theme

1 Put these events from the story in the correct order.

1	2	3	4	5	6	7	8	9	10	11	12	13
e												

a) Zeca annoyed Clara when she was on her own at the dance party.

b) Bruno met Clara when she went to the kiosk to buy coconut water.

c) Bruno and Clara started dating.

d) Zeca 'invited' Bruno to take part in his plan to steal and sell exams.

e) Bruno saw a movie called *Dead Poets Society* which profoundly impressed him.

f) Bruno and Clara passed the university entrance exams and also got a full scholarship and a grant.

g) Bruno took Clara to a *baile funk* dance party in the favela.

h) Bruno met Clara's father in a posh restaurant.

i) Bruno got his first job selling coconuts and coconut water at a small kiosk in Ipanema.

j) Zeca and his gang were arrested.

k) Clara went to the favela to meet Bruno's family.

l) Zeca's bodyguards took Bruno to see him.

m) Bruno went to the police with recorded evidence of the plan.

2 Listen and check your answers.

3 **Make a list of the places that are mentioned in the story. Why are they important?**

4 **For a story to be plausible (= likely to be true) factual information must be accurate. Find examples of specific details in the story which are realistic and authentic.**

5 **Write a short summary of the basic plot of the story. Use linking words like the ones below to connect your text. You can use exercise 1 to help you.**

> first   then   then one day   finally   next   after that
>
> the following day   two days / one week etc. later
>
> but   so   after a very short time   sometime later
>
> soon   soon after   as soon as

6 **What ideas or messages are there in the story? Give examples to support your answer. Below are a few suggestions to help you start.**

a) We are responsible for our own lives, and we can change things.

b) Dating people of different races and from different backgrounds is perfectly acceptable.

c) It is important to have clear principles about what is right and wrong.

7 **Write a short summary of the events in the story by retelling it from the point of view of one of the characters.**

After Reading

Language

1 Complete the dialogues with the sentences below.

a) **A:** Come on Bruno, I have customers waiting!
   B: ....

b) **A:** You should be studying hard!
   B: ....

c) **A:** Oh, I'm sorry! I didn't see you there.
   B: ....

d) **A:** I love reading and I don't think it's a waste of time!
   B: ....

e) **A:** I could meet you here at about six fifteen.
   B: ....

f) **A:** OK, it's a deal!
   B: ....

g) **A:** Where are you?
   B: ....

h) **A:** Hiya! I'm not late, am I?
   B: ....

i) **A:** So what do you do, Bruno?
   B: ....

j) **A:** Do you mind?
   B: ....

1 Great! So I'll see you later then.
2 Of course not.
3 No way! You're kidding me, right?
4 No, you're right on time.
5 Oh, give me a break!
6 So, let's shake on it!
7 Okay, I'm coming!
8 I work.
9 I'm here, dad! Calm down!
10 It's OK, no problem.

2 **Choose the correct alternative to fill in the spaces in the sentences. Write 1, 2 or 3 in the space.**

a) Here they're only .... detectives and law enforcement agencies, but anybody can buy them on the Internet.

1 used by   **2** use for   **3** using by

b) "You'll .... it," his friend said, laughing. "Now stop messing about with the collar."

1 get use to   **2** get using to   **3** get used to

c) That's what they .... abandoned street kids in the past.

1 usually to call   **2** are use to calling   **3** used to call

d) He and his gang also controlled the games of football the boys .... on a small piece of open land in the favela.

1 usually play   **2** used to play   **3** were used playing

3 **Match the adjectives on the left with the nouns on the right to produce the most natural-sounding combination. Make sentences with the words.**

a) ☐ foolproof   **1** mood
b) ☐ sheer   **2** track
c) ☐ first   **3** second
d) ☐ menacing   **4** steps
e) ☐ fast   **5** panic
f) ☐ bad   **6** smile
g) ☐ stabbing   **7** idea
h) ☐ split   **8** plan
i) ☐ broad   **9** impression
j) ☐ steep   **10** look
k) ☐ awkward   **11** pain
l) ☐ brilliant   **12** silence

After Reading
Exit Test

1 Tick (✔) T (true) or F (false).

	T	F
a) Bruno lived in an apartment block near Ipanema beach.	☐	☐
b) A film called "Carpe Diem" opened Bruno's eyes to new ways of thinking.	☐	☐
c) Clara and Bruno met for the first time at a kiosk on the beach front.	☐	☐
d) Clara and Bruno helped each other to study for the university entrance exams.	☐	☐
e) Bruno wanted to study math at university.	☐	☐
f) Pedro found it difficult to deal with Clara after her mother died.	☐	☐
g) Pedro was very happy when he found out that Clara was dating Bruno.	☐	☐
h) Bruno arrived late at the restaurant when he went to meet Pedro for the first time.	☐	☐
i) Bruno's mother was a single mother with three children.	☐	☐
j) Clara had a wonderful time at the dance party.	☐	☐
k) Zeca planned to steal the university entrance exams and use Bruno and Clara to sell them.	☐	☐
l) Bruno secretly videoed the gang of thieves and took the evidence to the police.	☐	☐
m) All the thieves were killed in the police raid.	☐	☐
n) Bruno and Clara passed the university entrance exams.	☐	☐
o) Bruno, Clara and their families organized a celebration party in the favela.	☐	☐

2 With a partner correct the false sentences.

3 Read the text below and choose the correct word for each space. Write 1, 2, or 3 in the space.

Bruno was slim and good-looking with **(a)** .... , jet-black hair and sparkling, dark brown **(b)** .... He had a very distinctive, **(c)** ....
voice. That was also pleasant and cheerful and warm. But he didn't use his voice to win **(d)** .... over. No, whenever Bruno **(e)** .... anything, it was always relevant and meaningful. His classmates at school teased him about being **(f)** .... , but Bruno never got embarrassed or nervous; it was just the way he was. He kept himself to **(g)** ....
And only spoke when he had something to say. Oh, and he had one of those irresistible smiles that light up your day. And he constantly looked on the **(h)** .... side of things and was optimistic **(i)** ....
everything. Quite **(j)** .... , he was a nice happy guy and you couldn't help but like him.

a) **1** short   **2** low   **3** small

b) **1** eyelashes   **2** eyelids   **3** eyes

c) **1** steep   **2** deep   **3** big

d) **1** people   **2** persons   **3** peoples

e) **1** spoke   **2** talked   **3** said

f) **1** shy   **2** rude   **3** genuine

g) **1** him   **2** his self   **3** himself

h) **1** bright   **2** light   **3** cool

i) **1** with   **2** by   **3** about

j) **1** surely   **2** simply   **3** actually

After Reading
Projects

WEB 1 **Favelas**

a) **According to the United Nations, in Brazil between 20% and 30% of the urban population live in favelas. With a partner, research the subject of favelas in Brazil on the Internet. Then tell the class.**

For suggestions check the links on the Helbling Readers website.

b) **Write a short, personal account about life in a favela from the point of view of one of the people living there.**

WEB 2 **Cyber-bullying**

Wikipedia explains that cyber-bullying "involves the use of information and communication technologies to support deliberate, repeated, and hostile behaviour by an individual or group, that is intended to harm others."

With a partner research the subject of cyber-bullying on the Internet. Compare this to traditional bullying. Find out about the dangers of this kind of bullying and suggest some possible solutions. Then tell the class.